ALL THE HOLLOW PLACES

poems by

Molly Beth Griffin

Finishing Line Press
Georgetown, Kentucky

ALL THE HOLLOW PLACES

ACKNOWLEDGMENTS

Many thanks to Deborah Keenan, Tasslyn Magnusson, Susan Marie
Swanson, Kathryn Kysar, Bao Phi, and E. Kristin Anderson—poetry
champions, all.

Publisher: Leah Maines
Editor: Christen Kincaid
Cover Art: Emer Griffin
Author Photo: Bao Phi
Cover Design: Leah Huete

Printed in the USA on acid-free paper.
Order online: www.finishinglinepress.com
also available on amazon.com

Author inquiries and mail orders:
Finishing Line Press
P. O. Box 1626
Georgetown, Kentucky 40324
U. S. A.

Table of Contents

Ivy and Spirea at the Winter Solstice

Winter vines cling,
twist, tangle, bind to branches.

Suddenly stripped bare of leaves,
all the dark green modesty
of their embrace
turned to flame and shed.

And now, here,
before a bright blue December sky,
their yearlong love affair is revealed.

In the frigid wind
they grasp each other close
hiding nothing.

What can I hold that tightly
before the clear eyes
of the whole windswept world?

The Discovery

A paleontologist in China found a piece of amber
the size of a dried apricot and bought it
from a jewelry maker at a market stall in Myanmar—

a piece of amber with
a dinosaur tail frozen inside.

The creature was once sparrow-sized and
"could have danced on the palm of your hand."
That should be incredible enough, but no:
this tail had feathers still attached.

This tail had feathers still attached,
and now the whole world is redrawing
its imagination.

Agates

I brought my agate collection along
when I went to visit my son's second
grade class. I divided it up: gave each
table a bowl of rocks and a magnifying
glass, told them agates form mostly from
ancient lava where gas bubbles once left
hollow places. Over time, molecules filled
those empty spaces with intricate layers of
color, concentric bands unique to each rock.

The wonder on their faces
as they gasped over each
tiny glowing pebble
started to fill in
all the hollow
places
in me.
Their awe
found all my empty
spaces (where my fear
lives, my doubt and worry)
and began to lay down layers
of beauty and light there instead.

The Rise

I'm planning a trip to see the Sandhill Cranes migrate
through the Platt River Valley with my son. He is seven
and so I will have to convince them, the birders, that he
can be quiet and calm enough to hide in the bird blind
and wait for the rise, and watch through binoculars,
and listen to the din of the birds waking, pecking the ice
off their legs. I hope they let him come, because he'd love
to see it, so many thousands of birds taking to the air together.
He is not like most children. He can't control his body, can't
stay on his feet in the grocery store—but he can wait stock
still for a bunny to hop across the yard toward him, and
I know the cranes would stun him silent.

The one time I saw it, the migration, I was pregnant with him.
I zipped a giant down coat over my belly, round with him,
and went to watch the birds with my mother, before dawn,
in near blizzard conditions. Half the roads were detoured.
I did not know, before I saw it, how it could possibly be worth
the trek, in the snow and wind. But most things that are hard
and slow are worth it in the end, and memory graciously wipes
clean most of the 63 hours of my first labor, most of the drive
to the bird sanctuary in the dark, most of the hardest slowest
parts of life. But you never forget the rise—the thousands
upon thousands of wingbeats circling to the sky. You never
forget the baby lifted to your chest—heartbeat wild, baby bird
mouth searching, feathered body folded against your skin.
You rise to meet that child, and the hours fall away behind you.

So I will book the hotel room, reserve our spots at the sanctuary,
lie about his age if I have to. We will drive through three states
to get there. The birds are migrating now, their long journey
has already begun and this time I want him to see it for himself.

For April

In the middle of
all this—the endless scandals,
the rumbles of war,
the refugees turned away
at the door—
500,000 people tune in
to the live cam.
We've heard the news: a hoof!
April the giraffe might give birth
today, so overdue,
and we're all desperate
for a miracle, a spotted
savior, a gangly,
six foot tall,
long-eyelashed
baby
in a barn
to save us from
our sins.

Marked

It is so human, don't you think,
to try to cover up the city's neon green
spray-painted X on the bark of an old
tree? To say, no please, not yet, give us
another year with this one.

But of course, they have to take down
old, sick trees in the city, so they don't fall
on people's houses or power lines.
They will plant new healthy baby
trees in their places.

And yet still, we can't help but cling
to the deep-grooved skin of these old
beauties. They've seen so much pass
down our busy streets, year after
year. It's right to treasure that, to scribble
out the green paint with black and hope
the chainsaw will pass this one by.

Sunday Morning

The lake is dotted
with a hundred small black coots:
live pointillism.

Loon fishes alone
on the other side, her breast
contains a hundred

white speckles in itself.
She is her own flock.

What My Prayers Look Like
(with thanks to warsan shire)

The other mom at our bus stop
is afraid to wait on the corner
with her children,
worried immigration
will swoop in,
take her away.

My son draws ocelots and beavers,
writes letters about the border wall
and the pipelines to send to our senators,
to the president. We correct his spelling
together, but I leave his 'plees'
in its childlike form.
This is what my prayers
look like, now.

Later I'm afraid to scroll through
the news— school shootings, reefs
destroyed, another bomb dropped.
Where do I press my hands
to make the bleeding stop?

I'll just elevate the whole gushing world
above my heart
and hope
it's not too late.

Ode to a Hollow Tree

A city arborist told me once, pointing with two smudged
fingers, that our silver maple in the backyard was 'topped'
back when chainsaws and cherry pickers were new.
They started hacking the canopies off all the big trees
and so now it's hollow. "Still looks healthy," he said,
"but definitely hollow. Leave the green. It needs all
its green." Then he chided me for planting the catalpa
too deep and he was on his way.

This morning I watch my hollow tree and think
how typical it is to shake our heads at old
decisions. How could they have done such a thing
just because they could? But of course, we do
that all the time. Act rashly. Then later, we blame. We
regret so much.

I swore at my children this morning, while they fought
at the breakfast table. I screamed at them, said such
terrible things. They just wouldn't stop. They never
stop. It goes on and on, but how could I have done
such a thing just because I could? Later, I
regret so much.

There are squirrels nesting inside my hollow tree.
Woodpeckers love the feast of bugs it provides.
And this morning, after I walked my son to the bus
stop, dropped my daughter at preschool, I came
back home to this hollow tree, this monument
to mistakes, and there was a cardinal singing
in its weathered branches. It chose this tree,
despite its deep imperfections. Or because of them.

Maybe if my children could choose,
they'd choose me
anyway
too.

Escape

Last night our pop tent blew away.
I was supposed to fold it
and tuck it behind the back door
but it wouldn't fold, and so
I left it out there in the back yard
kind of wedged between
the jungle gym and the house.

After the kids were in bed
I went out to get it
and it wasn't there.
I swept a flashlight across our yard,
then leaned over the fence
and scanned the other yards too—
but it was gone.

This morning a neighbor sent a picture,
showing me where it ended up.
It had blown almost two blocks,
crossed a busy city street.

I imagined it venturing out—
was it timid and afraid?
Or bold and laughing as it rolled
like tumbleweed? Did it sneak
around corners? Or charge
down the middle of the road?
Did it vault fences? Hurdle cars?
Did it revel in the escape?
Or did it wish for home?

I must go out now, in the rain,
and bring back our prodigal tent.
I must try, again, to fold it
into itself, tuck it
into the small space
where it belongs.

Gather

We wade down the sidewalk,
ankle deep in autumn gold.
My daughter stops every step or two, stoops
to gather more leaves into the pom-poms
bursting from her small fists. Her pockets
bulge and crackle when she moves.

They don't need to be perfect
for her to want them.
Some are speckled brown,
some splitting apart, but
all are beautiful
to her.

Love Song for a Sparrow

Her sneakers patter down the zoo's tropics trail
past the lemurs and the komodo dragon,
past the pair of swinging gibbons
whose raucous love song echoes
through the trees. She is oblivious
to all this drama because a sparrow
has flown in from the Minnesota winter
through layers and layers of sliding doors
and it has flitted across her path.
Now she squeals in happiness
and pursues it.

Who's to say what creature deserves
my daughter's love song of raucous laughter
and the wet warmth of the tropics trail in winter?

She is the one who knows that beauty
does not have to be flashy, or rare.
It can be small and gray-brown,
quick and clever, and as out of place
here in paradise as we are.

Who Do You Want To Be?

Are you Captain Jack Sparrow,
or Barbossa? How wicked
are you feeling today?
Down to your bones?

Which Powerpuff Girl
is your favorite? Because I've always liked
Buttercup, but I know I'm really more
of a Blossom/Bubbles mix,
more sugar than spice.

Let's play Professor X
and Magneto, and see who wins.
Fine be Rogue. You always
want to be Rogue.

If I kill you with
my wooden sword
my sparkle dust
my mind tricks
the touch of my fingertips,
I promise I'll let you get up
and kill me back.

We'll play powerful
until we feel it
zinging magnetic
down to our wicked
bones, until our hair
turns white
and we're immortal.

Things I Have Stolen

In first grade I stole a book. A terrible, nonsensical learn-to-read book of stapled-together pages that I snuck home and hid in the bottom of a toy box under my bed. I don't know why I needed to possess this thing. We had other books. Better books. I was not a deprived child. But this thing, I kept. Secret. Hidden.

Later, I took a doll. It was a German doll from my grandparents' house. A small, precious thing that lived high on a bookshelf. She had wire in her limbs that made them bend just a little and a traditional dress of bright colors. I was allowed to play with her when I was there. One day I took her. I don't remember the details of the stealing. But after that, I had her in my dresser at home, tucked away.

This might be a coincidence, that the two things I secreted away for myself as a child were a book and a doll from the home country, but I don't think so. Children know things. They know that there are parts of themselves that they should take and tuck away, things they should guard as precious. I wonder if, as an adult, I have the audacity to take what I think I need, protect the pieces of myself that sometimes need to be hidden away from the world.

I don't know if I'm brash enough to steal things, anymore, even a small stapled book, worthless to anyone else, even a wire girl on a high shelf saying "I am you, I am you, please keep me safe."

Inside memory

I remember the loops
of brown carpet beneath my fingers
and then later, it was blue, and shorter,
when shag went out of fashion
but I still played low-to-the-ground
games and spent long afternoons
in the cool, dark stillness of my house,
sprawled there, on the living room floor,
rolling marbles through wrapping
paper tubes, running masking tape down
the center for balloon volleyball,
inventing tumbling routines and dealing
so many hands of solitaire. Yes, I think
children know carpet like their own skin.

Somehow the distance, now,
between my body and the ground
has become miles
and I don't know the texture
of anywhere.

LENORE

My daughter makes the E's
in her name
with lots of shelves
room for plenty of books
and toys and stuffies,
floor to ceiling.
However tall
that initial backbone reaches,
however many shelves fit there,
that's how many belong
on each E.

They will correct her
in Kindergarten.
They will take down her extra shelves
so that each E has just three.
I know this is important,
in the long run.

But for now,
I love that LENORE
can design herself
and make space
for everything.

Clearly

You search for seed pods,
thorns, patterns of bark and moss—
small precious shapes that get over
looked when people search for beauty.
You zoom in close but the wind
keeps snatching the focus
away.

It's not even windy today,
but any breath can shake
these dry branches
—seed pods are designed
to rattle loose in the breeze, so
it doesn't take
much. It doesn't take much
to capture it except

a willingness to crouch in the snow
and try again
and again to find the sharp outlines
of small things, brown and gray against
brown and gray
and white.

It doesn't take much
to capture it except
an insistence that beauty is worth
waiting for, and a belief that the world
will, at some point, for a brief moment,
hold its breath

and let you
see it

clearly.

Liberty

A man dances on the street corner
in a crown and robe, Liberty
Tax on a sash across his chest.

We pay our taxes to guard
the gilded penthouse of the president,
build more jets with bellies full
of bombs. Pipelines crisscross our rivers
and we know they're poisoning people
on purpose. I want to pay my taxes
anyway, because my son's teacher
deserves to be paid, this street's
potholes need fixing.

The man dances for minimum wage
and I don't know if his smile is real
or not, but it looks real from here,
and I think, maybe he's happy.
Maybe in spite of everything,
in this one bright moment,
this is what liberty
looks like: dancing
on Lake Street and Cedar Avenue,
in the sunshine.

Close

We found a dead sparrow
on the sidewalk.
My eyes darted away;
my son bent down to look close.
"Don't touch," I told him
but he wanted to look and look,
and I said he could come out later
and look again when I sent his other
mom out to clean it up.

He ran outside the moment she came home,
they were gone a long time.

Later, she said she let him touch
it because aside from its too-loose neck
it was somehow still perfect.
She said they fanned out its gray-brown wings
together, and felt its tiny claw feet,
and then he cupped it gently in his hands,
so soft and so light and so real.

My eyes filled up when she told me this,
at the tenderness of that image,
at his curiosity, at his compassion.
My eyes filled up because I'd missed all that life
for being squeamish of death.

I walk wide
so I don't have to look too close,
and I miss so much.

Snow Bird

This morning a robin perched
on the peak of my neighbor's powder-
covered roof
and surveyed the April
landscape.

It was spring
yesterday.

It will be spring again
tomorrow.

This snow will melt
so fast
we'll forget
the sinking grief
of this
long
moment.

I don't know if the robin
remembers
that this happens every
year.

Nothing ever moves forward,
turning and turning toward the light,
without sliding backward
into winter
once or twice.

What Hearts Do

The bleeding hearts
are bursting through
the ribs of fence
around a neighbor's yard,
spilling their blossoms
in wide pink arcs
over the sidewalk.

Because that is what hearts
do—push past all barriers,
break through the armor
we build around them, to show
others our beauty, and pain.

The garden inside
will find a way
to share itself
with the world.

Shadow Spotting

I saw a shadow move at my feet
and knew, somehow, it was a bird's shadow
so I turned toward the sun expecting a big crow
or something equally ordinary in the bare
branches of these late-winter trees.

I didn't think I'd see an owl
settling its dense feathers, swiveling
its curious head toward me,
and away.

It grew weary of my company and shook
itself into the bright air.
A few slow wing beats
and it was lost to me, its shadow
whisked across the forest floor.

But not lost for long.
Soon I found it again, hunkered
in another tree, blending in,
nearly invisible despite its size.

I wonder how many times my eyes
have skipped over a strangely mottled branch
overhead, or missed the movement of a shadow,
roughed out on the ground.

At least today, I turned toward the sun
and looked up, and so today I left feeling
lucky.

It was like that owl had spotted me, from way up there.
It was like that shadow had chosen to glide down here
and touch my feet.

Crown Shyness

Did you know
some species of trees
as they reach up
and up,
hold their crowns
close, hesitate
to touch the branches
of their neighbors.
Look up:
they make a canopy
of green puzzle pieces
with channels of blue sky
trickling through.

Maybe it looks like
standoffishness,
because we like the romance
of entwined branches,
but no—
these are trees that say
there is space here
for all of us,
and enough light
to go around.

Eclipsed

(after Path of Totality by Laura Bradley Rede)

Nazis are marching, wielding torches.
Hate is unhooded now, it burns openly
on the internet, at the dinner table,
in the streets.

And even though this is nothing new,
it feels sudden to some of us, and so we turn
desperately to love, and our candles try
to burn as bright as torches.

A week from now the moon will pass
in front of the sun, and draw a stripe
of darkness across America.

And maybe people were already looking
for eclipse glasses before
the night the Nazis marched,
but it felt like the rush came after that.
Now everyone is scrambling
for a way to look directly
at the sun
without going blind,
for a way to witness this
with their eyes open.

We all need to know if it's possible
for light (and love, and hope)
to be eclipsed—
and then for light
(and love, and hope)

to return.

My Selkie

She chases each wave,
forgets always the icy
crash coming back
to tackle her.

Maybe she wants the sea to win.
Maybe it's a dance.
Maybe part of her remembers
having fins,
and gills,
salt lips
and scale skin.
Maybe she's just trying
to go home
and the ocean has to remind
her: look, you have legs
for running, lungs
for laughing.
You'd miss the way the wind
combs your sand-
colored hair.

Sentinel

A toy tiger figurine stalks the ledge
of my bath tub.
She's been there for months.
The kids have moved on to playing dragons
in the tub, but I haven't moved her.
I don't know why.
I shower in her presence in the mornings;
bathe under her watchful eye in the evenings.
I can hide nothing
from her. In this vulnerable
place, she is my silent
sentinel.

We all laugh sometimes
about how long she's been there,
but still I do not toss her in the toy bin.
When she topples from the ledge
I pick her up, and put her
back.
Every time.

I guess I like
the idea that something fierce,
something fanged and clawed,
paces my bathroom
day and night,
heedless of the grout that needs
scrubbing and the nearly-empty
shampoo bottles I keep forgetting
to rinse out.

I guess I like
the idea that this striped guardian
will find the edges
of anywhere,
and walk them.
We all need to claim
some imperfect territory
as our own, maybe even decide
our imperfect selves
are worth protecting.

Morning on Lake Superior

Wake up to a rainbow striped sky,

a new skim of ice on the lake,

and fresh tracks in the snow,
a woodland Braille that reads
some quiet creature was here
in the night.

You are lucky to be sharing
this slice of earth
with something
so gentle
as that.

Stealing the Sea Nettle from the Omaha Zoo

Some people would take an elephant,
something grand. Maybe something cute, a sloth
to wear slung around the neck, warm forever.

I would steal a jellyfish.
I would take the biggest
and most beautiful sea nettle in the tank.

No I would not carry in an aquarium under cover
of night, fish it out with a green net like a dime goldfish.
I would swallow it—no not eat it—just slip
it safely down my throat and walk away.

I am water
and I want it to live inside of me, float
here in the brine of me.

My breath, my pulse
would slow to match the leisurely throb of
its movement,

its tentacles
winding and unwinding
their ropes and frills casually around
my ribs.

It would drape my spine
in its impossible fractals
and it would not sting me, but
together we would be electric.

Together we'd be nothing but inhale and exhale.

Zookeepers would just stand there, watching
the gentle pulse of us

as we moved steadily
through this busy sea of people,

and out into the bright
afternoon,

uncaught.

Birth Stories, 2009 & 2013

Recover (verb):
1) to return to a normal state of health, mind, or strength.
2) to find or regain possession of (something lost or stolen).

2009

You are being born. Your arrival is the opposite
of what we expected, planned, longed for. Wires bind
me to a slab of a bed, the light is harsh, a stranger
is catching you. The labor was too long, I was too tired,
the pain was too much, you were too big, we could not
meet you at home, after all.

The relief is huge when you are outside of me,
squirming at last on my chest, slick and separate, but
the rage is huge too. We were robbed of that perfect
experience the videos promised. My body is a ship-
wreck. Your face is purple with bruises. We don't
recover for a long time.

2013

You are being born. Your arrival is the opposite
of what we've come to expect, to fear, to dread. I almost
don't wake everyone in time. The midwife wastes
time packing, assuming she'd be with us three days,
again. But no—you rush through me in just
a few hours. The pain is bigger than my body can
contain but somehow I expand beyond it, I am
borderless.

We meet you at home, kneeling, at dawn. You drop
into the same hands that measured you, week by week.
The relief is huge. You crawl up my belly and latch
on and I laugh because you are eight pounds and two
minutes old and you know just what to do. Then I sob
at the wave of after pains you've triggered—my body
trying to shrink back into the shape of before.

But there is no going back, and I may never recover.
I don't recognize my hills and valleys, all my lines
are redrawn. We are a new country, now.

Wings

A monarch's wings
are all wadded up
when they first emerge
from the chrysalis,
before the fluid surges
in through the veins,
before the summer air
dries them out.

Anyone can tell
they're going to be beautiful,
stained-glass perfection,
as soon as the butterfly
can get them sorted out.

What if the monarch
looked at those crumpled
wings, those unflying wings,
those wet, failed wings
and said,
"never mind."

Molly Beth Griffin is the author of the award winning young adult novel *Silhouette of a Sparrow* (Milkweed Editions, 2012) as well as two picture books: *Loon Baby* (Houghton Mifflin Harcourt, 2011) and *Rhoda's Rock Hunt* (Minnesota Historical Society Press, 2014).

Her novel was featured on the ALA Rainbow List and the Amelia Bloomer List of Feminist Literature, was a Foreword Book of the Year, and received the Milkweed Prize for Children's Literature. Her picture books have won a Jeanette Fair Book Award, a NE Minnesota Book Award, and a Star of the North nomination. Her writing has also been awarded two Minnesota Arts Board grants, and a McKnight Fellowship. Molly is a graduate of Hamline University's MFA program in Writing for Children and Young Adults, and a teaching artist at The Loft Literary Center

Finishing Line Press published her first chapbook of poems, *Under Our Feet* in the spring of 2018. She lives in South Minneapolis with her partner and their two young children.

www.ingramcontent.com/pod-product-compliance
Lightning Source LLC
LaVergne TN
LVHW051610080426
835510LV00020B/3221